PIANO
Adventures® *by Nancy and Randall Faber*
THE BASIC PIANO METHOD

CONTENTS

FABER
PIANO ADVENTURES®
3042 Creek Drive
Ann Arbor, Michigan 48108

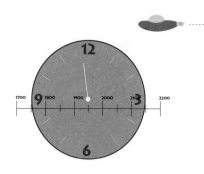

The Time Machine
(A Stop at the 18th Century)

Dynamic Check: Remember the *p* (piano)
and *f* (forte) signs!

Allegro moderato (moderately fast, ♩ = 108-120)

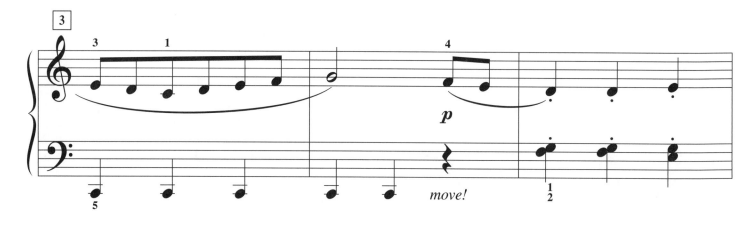

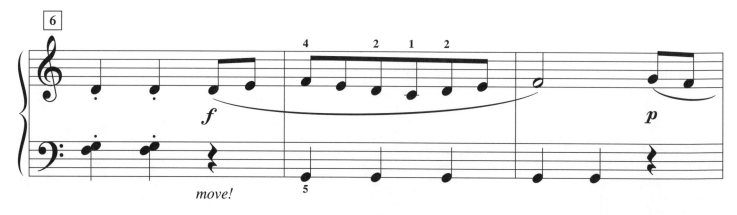

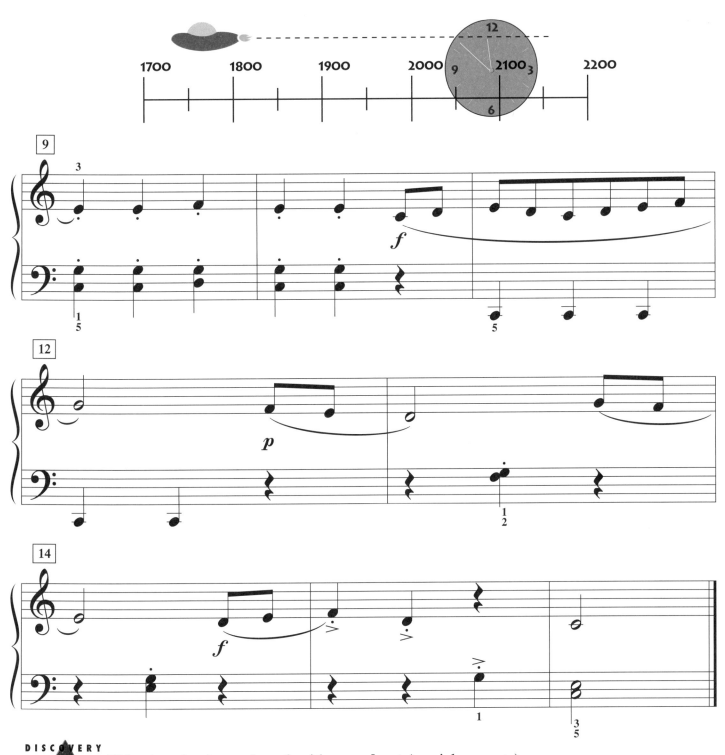

DISCOVERY

This piece begins on beat 3 with an **upbeat** (or pick-up note).
Tell your teacher what you know about an upbeat and an *incomplete last measure*.

Teacher Duet: (Student plays *as written*)

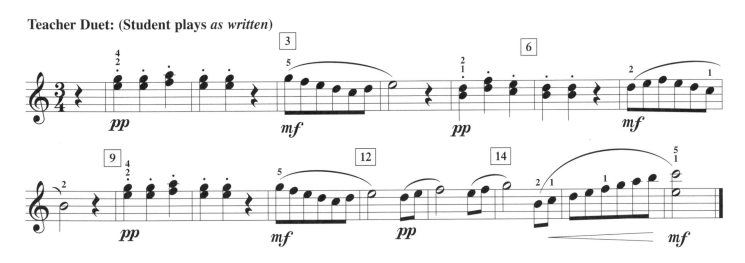

The Dragon Hunt

A Minor 5-Finger Scale

With energy (♩ = 108-132)

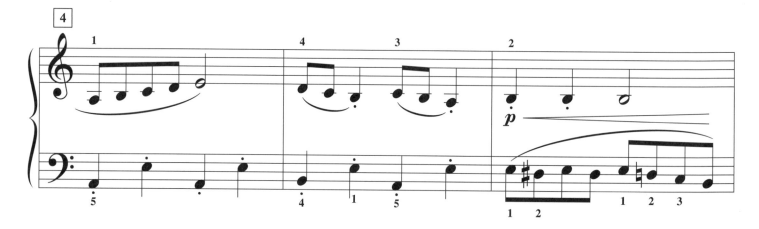

On repeat, jump to the
Special Ending,
measure 19.

📖 Lesson p.12 (Spanish Caballero)

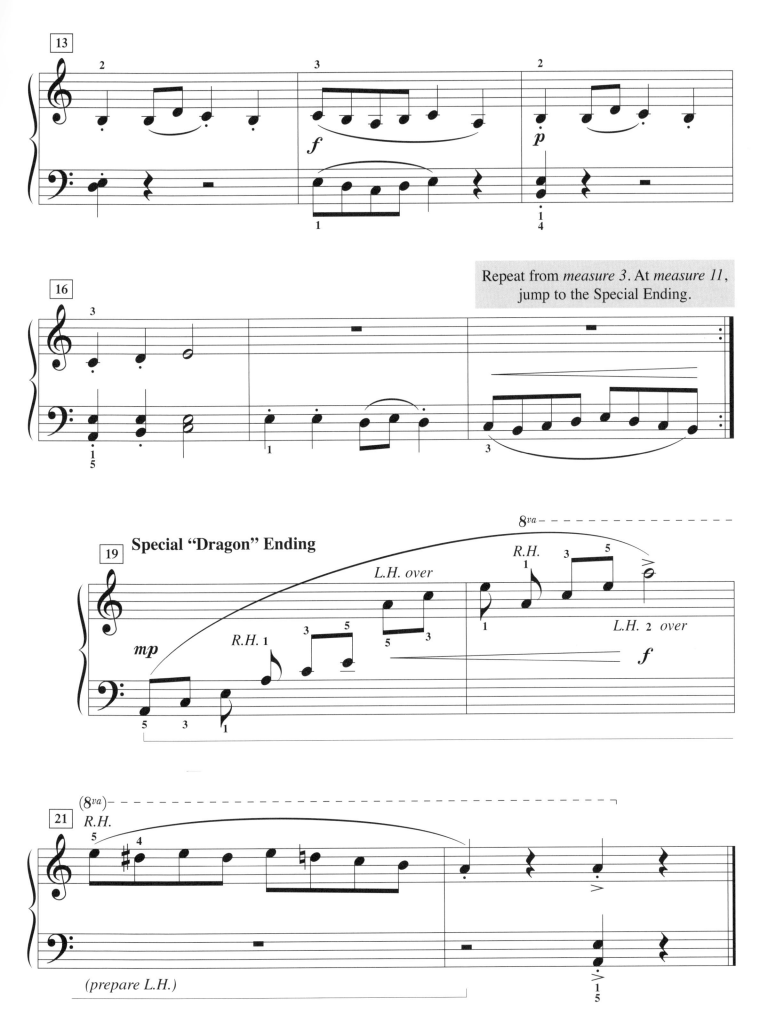

Repeat from *measure 3*. At *measure 11*,
jump to the Special Ending.

Special "Dragon" Ending

DISCOVERY

Be an adventurer! Can you *transpose* this piece to the **D minor 5-finger scale**?

Pagoda in the Purple Mist

Hold the right foot pedal down throughout the entire piece.

Flowing gently (♩ = 100-120)

Teacher Duet: (Student plays *1 octave higher*)

📖 Lesson p.18 (Shave and a Haircut)
FF10

DISCOVERY

Can you play this piece on all **black keys**? Move your hand position down a *half step*.

4
UNIT

A Day at the Carnival

Key of C Major

Cheerfully (♩ = 112-144)

Rides · · · and · · · priz · · · es

are · at · the · car - ni - val · fair. · I · see · a

roll · · · er · · · coast · · · er

Teacher Duet: (Student plays *1 octave higher*)

📖 Lesson p.22 (Jumpin' Jazz Cat) · FF10

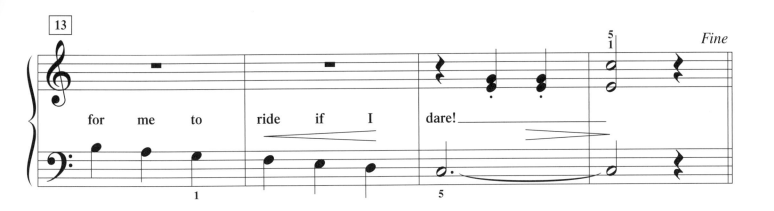

for me to ride if I dare!

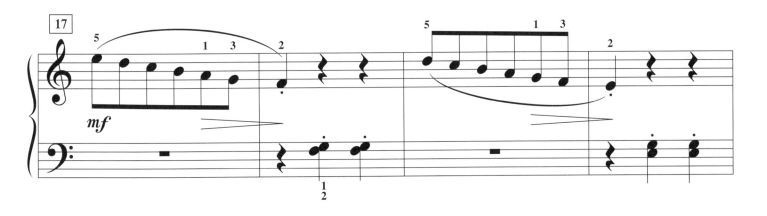

 DISCOVERY

Find the three R.H. **scale patterns**. Name the starting note of each pattern.
What do you notice about the fingering?

Sunburst Waltz

Key of _____ Major

Waltz Check: Can you play beats 2 and 3 *lighter* than beat 1?

Gracefully (♩ = 120-144)

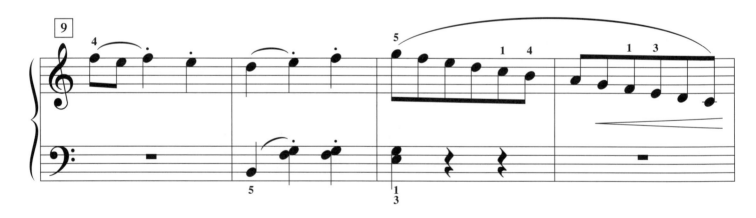

DISCOVERY Name the harmony in each measure for *measures 1-16* as **I** or **V7**.

Theme by Haydn*
Key of G Major

Franz Joseph Haydn
(1732-1809, Austria)
adapted

- First practice the R.H. alone for the quick shifts on the repeated notes.

Allegro (♩ = 108-132)

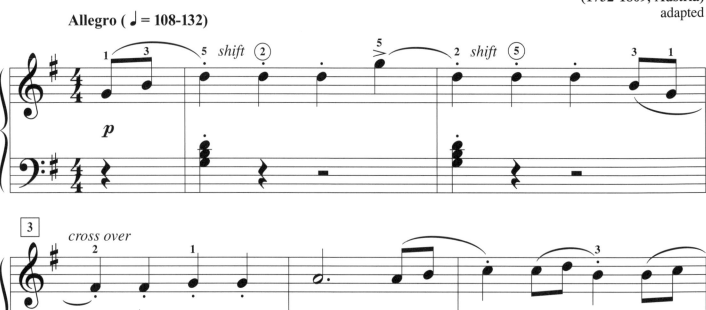

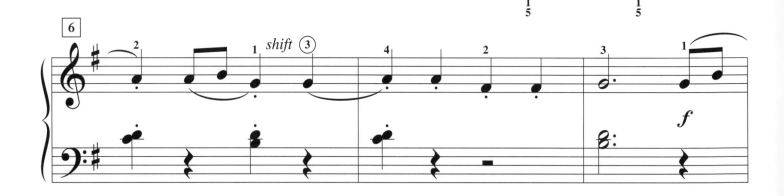

Teacher Duet: (Student plays *1 octave higher*)

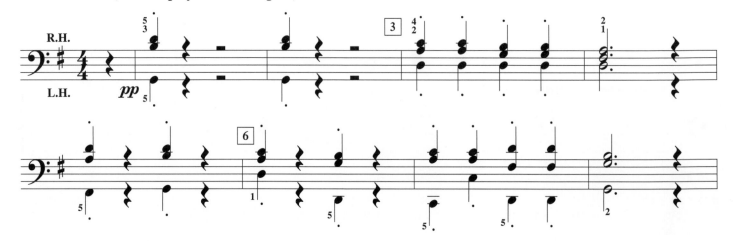

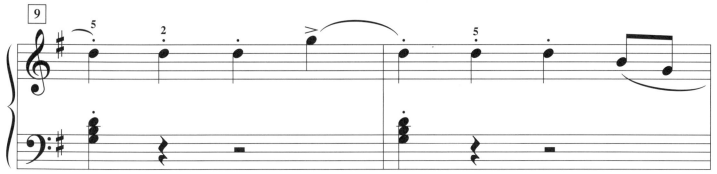

DISCOVERY Can you transpose *Theme by Haydn* to the key of **C major**?

6 UNIT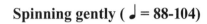

The Milky Way

Key of _____ Major

Spinning gently (♩ = 88-104)

L.H. 2 over to F♯

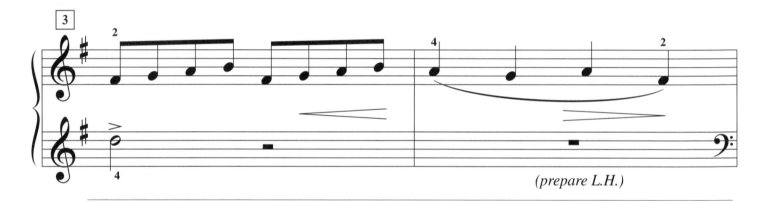

(prepare L.H.)

L.H. 2 over to E

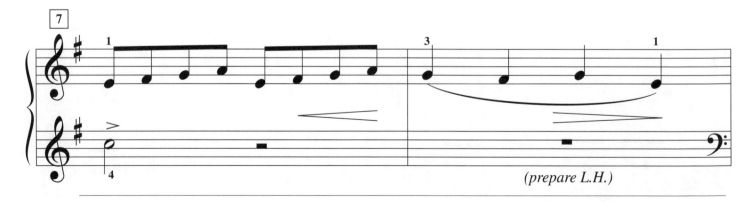

(prepare L.H.)

14   Lesson p.40 (Riding the Wind)   FF1080

Are you playing the F♯ in each chord?

DISCOVERY Does the R.H. begin on the *tonic*, *dominant*, or *leading tone* in the key of **G major**?

♪ = ♩

This piece is very old—written 400 years ago!
The L.H. 5ths imitate the steady drone of a bagpipe.

Dudelsack
(Bagpipes)

Unknown composer
(circa 1600)
original form

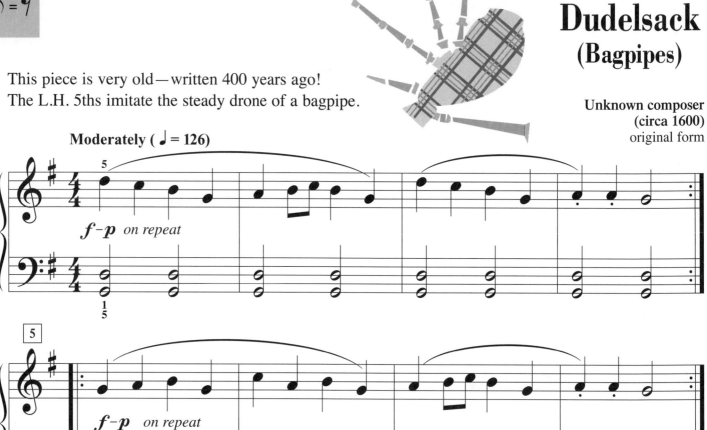

Here is a "rock" arrangement of the same piece.

- Listen to your teacher demonstrate the music.
  Imitate the rhythms you hear.

Rockin' Bagpipes

arranged by N. Faber

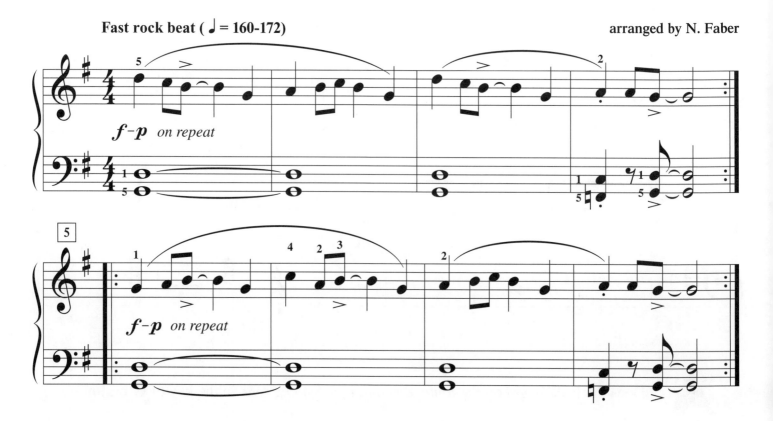

DISCOVERY

Which hand uses an **eighth rest**? On what beat does the eighth rest occur?

Kum Ba Yah
("Come By Here")

This piece will help you practice
graceful lifts across the keys.

Peacefully (♩ = 76-92)

Traditional African

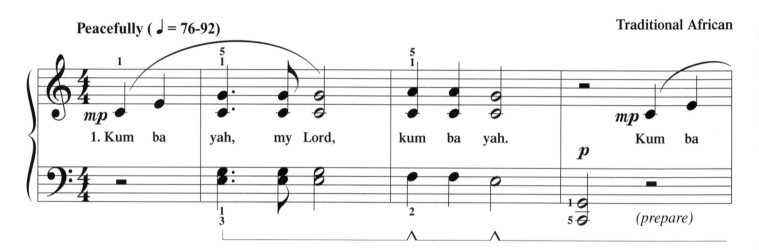

1. Kum ba yah, my Lord, kum ba yah. Kum ba

yah, my Lord, kum ba yah. Kum ba

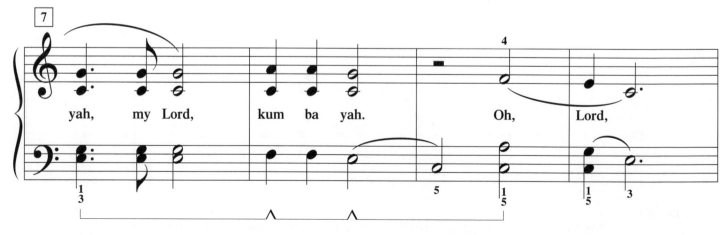

yah, my Lord, kum ba yah. Oh, Lord,

Additional lyrics

3. **Someone's sleeping, Lord, kum ba yah…**
4. **Someone's crying, Lord, kum ba yah…**
5. **Someone's praying, Lord, kum ba yah…**
6. **Someone's shouting, Lord, kum ba yah…**

Für Elise*

Ludwig van Beethoven
(1770–1827, Germany)
arranged

With motion (♩ = 92-108)

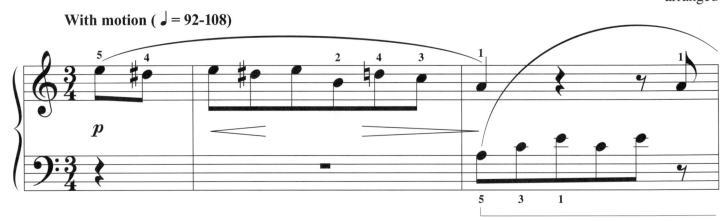

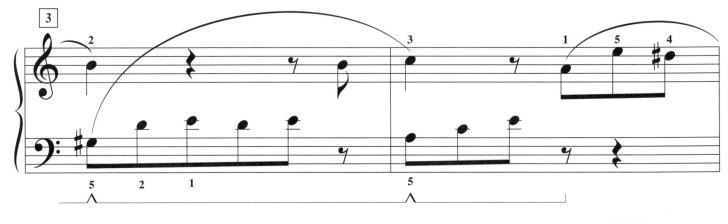

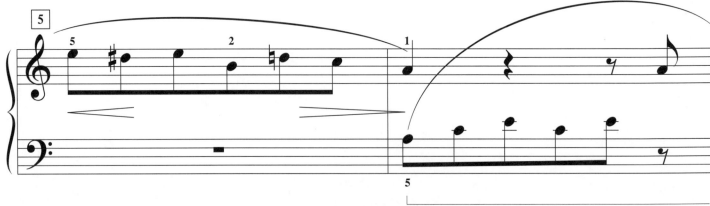

*__Note to Teacher:__ This simplification of Beethoven's famous Für Elise is included here for musical pleasure and pianistic development. It is not intended for competitions or festivals which designate only authentic keyboard repertoire.

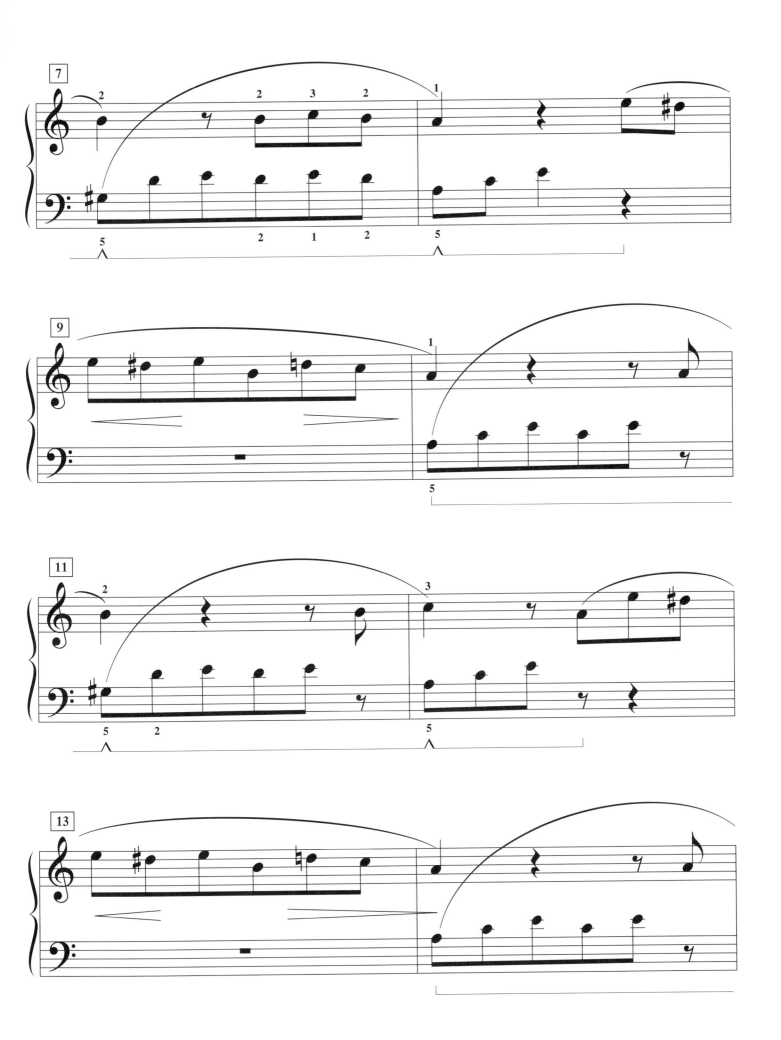

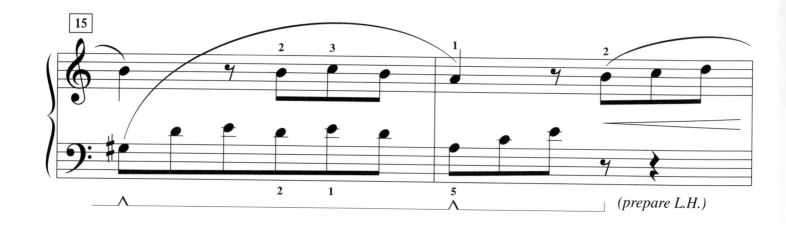

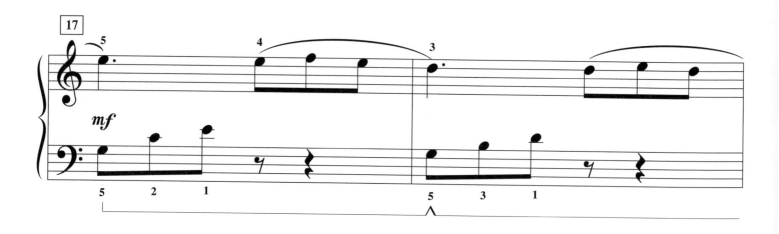

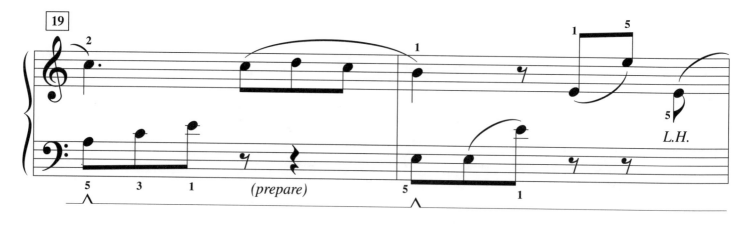

(Hint: the left, the right, the left, the right hand

22

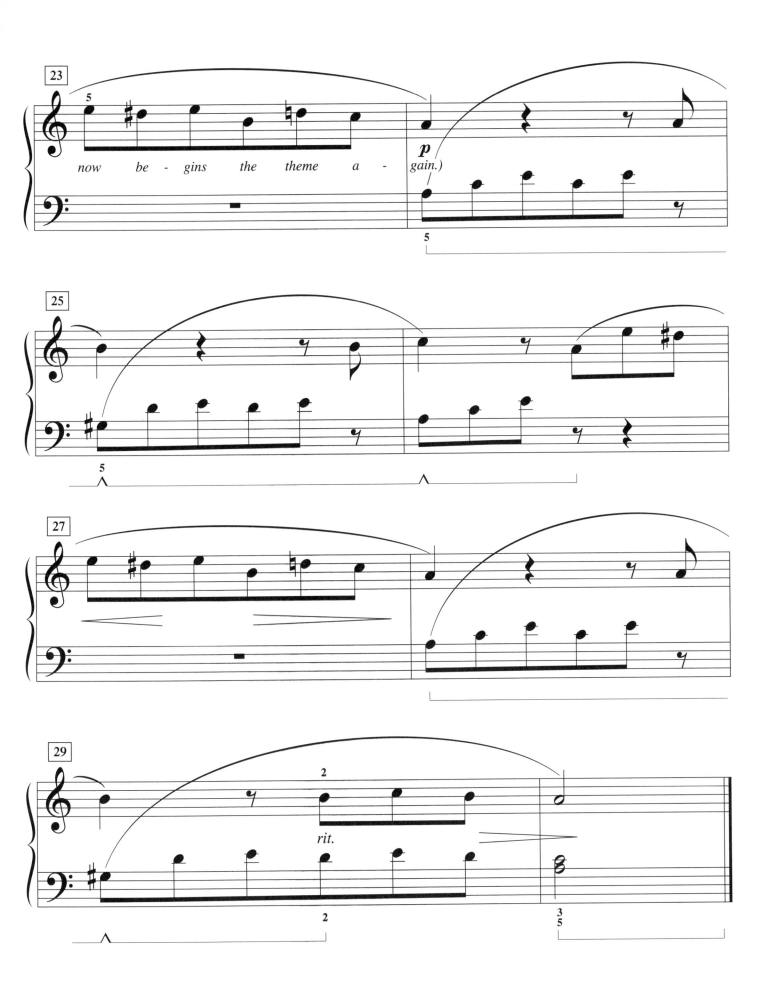

now be - gins the theme a - gain.)

DISCOVERY

Can you spell the name **Beethoven** correctly? Practice writing it until it's easy!

In My Red Convertible

Key of _____ Major

Cruising along (♩ = 88-100)

In my red con - vert - i - ble,

3
dream - y red con - vert - i - ble,

5
I'd be in the driv - er's seat,
(prepare L.H.)

7
cruis - in' down the cit - y street.
(prepare L.H.)

Get a bur-ger down on Main, cruise in, cruise

(prepare L.H.)

move

move

on.

DISCOVERY Where does the L.H. imitate the R.H.? Show your teacher.

Teacher Duet: (Student plays *as written*)

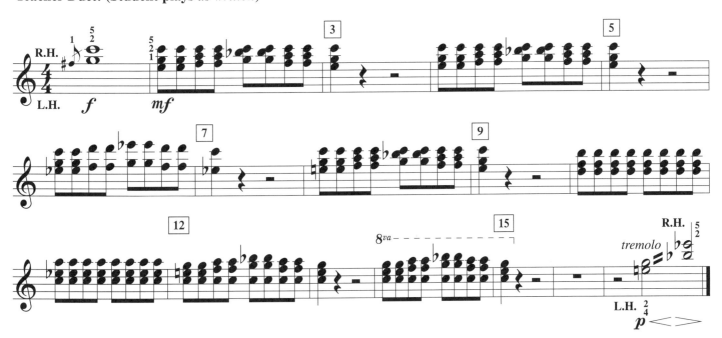

Everybody Loves Saturday Night

Key of _____ Major

Rather fast (♩ = 112-132)

Traditional

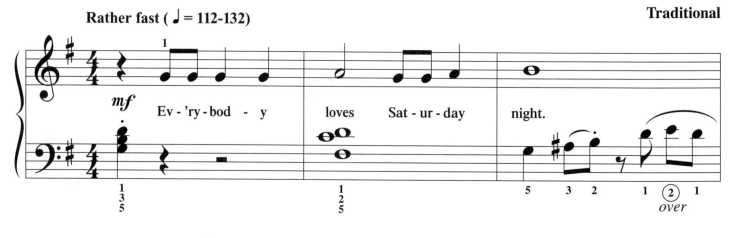

Ev - 'ry - bod - y   loves   Sat - ur - day   night.

over

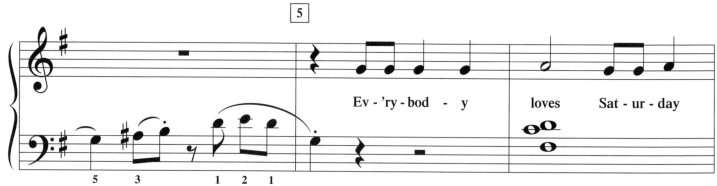

Ev - 'ry - bod - y   loves   Sat - ur - day

Teacher Duet: (Student plays *1 octave higher*)

🎵 Lesson pp.54-55 (Duke of York Strut)   FF101

night.

f Ev - 'ry - bod - y,

ev - 'ry - bod - y,   ev - 'ry - bod - y,   ev - 'ry - bod - y,

mf ev - 'ry - bod - y   loves____ Sat - ur - day   night.

DISCOVERY The **eighth rest** in this piece always occurs on:

beat 1   *beat 2*   *beat 3*   *beat 4*   (circle one)

- Learn both the *Secondo* and *Primo* parts.
- Have fun playing with a friend or your teacher.

The British Grenadiers
Secondo

Play BOTH HANDS *8va LOWER*.

With energy (♩ = 116-132)

Traditional

The natural cancels the B♭.

📖Lesson p.60 (Turkish March)

FF10

The British Grenadiers
Primo

Play BOTH HANDS *8va HIGHER*.

Traditional

With energy (♩ = 116-132)

The natural cancels the B♭.

Turn page!

71086

Secondo

Primo

The Banana Boat Song

Happy and carefree (♩ = 132-152)

Jamaican Folk Song

Teacher Duet: (Student plays *as written*)

📖 Lesson p.63 (Aria)

FF10

DISCOVERY

Point out the following in this piece:
I, **IV**, and **V7** chords in the key of F, eighth rest, fermata, and accent mark

Allegro!

A sonatina is an instrumental piece, often with three sections called movements. Each movement has a different character or mood. The **first movement** is *allegro*—cheerful and lively!

Classic Sonatina
1st Movement

Key of _____ Major

N. Faber

🎵 Lesson pp.66-71 (Scale and Chord Adventures)

FF10

Coda (the Italian word for "ending")

The **second movement** is slower and calmer.
The performer can "show off" their phrasing,
tone, and pedaling!

2nd Movement

Key of _____ **Major**

- Trace the key signature for the
  first page of music.

Andante...

Andante moderato (♩ = 100-116)

Presto!

The **third movement** of a sonatina is usually quite fast and rhythmic! As you play, create "super" staccatos, sharp accents, and colorful dynamics.

3rd Movement

Key of _____ Major

Presto (very fast, "in two," ♩ = 96-112)

FF10

cresc. poco a poco (little by little)

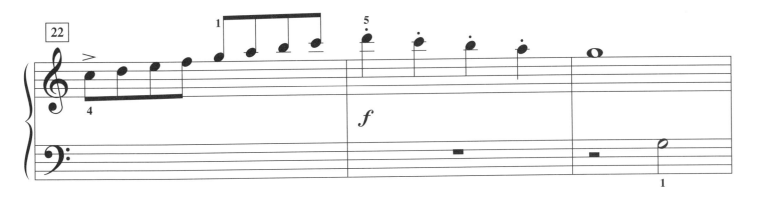

1086